Unlocking the Beauty of

The Catechism

The Creed: Part One

Christopher J. Ruff, S.T.L.

Unlocking the Beauty of the Catechism
The Creed: Part One

Novo Millennio Press
PO Box 160
La Crescent, MN 55947
www.novomill.com

Nihil obstat: Rev. Jesse D. Burish, S.T.L.
Censor Librorum

Imprimatur: William Patrick Callahan, OFM Conv.
Bishop of La Crosse
August 15, 2012

The *nihil obstat* and *imprimatur* are official declarations that a book or pamphlet is free of doctrinal or moral error. No implication is contained therein that those who have granted the *nihil obstat* and *imprimatur* agree with the contents, opinions, or statements expressed.

Unless otherwise noted, Scripture quotations are from the Catholic Edition of the Revised Standard Version of the Bible, copyright © 1965, 1966 National Council of the Churches of Christ in the United States of America. Used by permission. All rights reserved.

Excerpts from the English translation of the *Catechism of the Catholic Church* for use in the United States of America copyright © 1994, United States Catholic Conference, Inc. - Libreria Editrice Vaticana. Used with Permission.

Cover art:
Manuel Panselinos, *Christ Enthroned.*
Protaton church, Mount Athos, Greece, ca 1290.
Image compliments of skete.com.

Graphics and Design:
Alice J. Andersen
www.alicejandersen.com.

The Discipleship Series

Novo Millennio Press

Preface

Birth of the Catechism

"Youth in Boston and in Moscow both wear blue jeans. They listen and dance to the same music. In a world which becomes ever smaller... I propose a commission of cardinals for the preparation of a draft of a conciliar catechism which would be promulgated by the Pope after having consulted the bishops of the world."

This statement was delivered by Cardinal Bernard Law at the 1985 Extraordinary Synod of Bishops in Rome. I remember it vividly because I had the honor to serve as a Vatican translator from Italian for the English-speaking press at that synod. As a theology student in Rome in the 1980's, I had learned the language and was blessed to be hired for this role.

There were 165 bishops present at the synod, and they took turns making many statements, or "interventions" in Vatican parlance. But this one stood out—this call for a new catechism that would span all peoples and cultures. There had not been a universal catechism since the Council of Trent in the 16th century. I felt hope and excitement as I began typing Cardinal Law's statement in English, and it caused an immediate stir among the members of the press covering the synod.

More importantly, Pope John Paul II warmed to the idea. Within a few months he had appointed a commission of twelve cardinals, chaired by Cardinal Joseph Ratzinger (now Pope Benedict XVI), to begin work on the project. Six years and nine drafts later, on October 11, 1992, after much collaboration with the bishops of the whole world, Pope John Paul II ordered the publication of the *Catechism of the Catholic Church.*

The Catechism was first published in French in November of 1992, quickly followed by the Italian edition. I was directing adult faith formation at a large parish in Minneapolis at that time, and I promptly ordered a copy. When it arrived I was captivated by its beauty and couldn't wait to introduce it to the people of the parish. So I began writing small-group study materials in anticipation of the Catechism's publication in English, which, after some delays, came about in 1994. Subsequently, more than 300 of our parishioners would use those materials to accompany their reading of the Catechism.

Now, as we celebrate the 20th anniversary of the Catechism, I am happy to present these resources, significantly revised and expanded, for the Year of Faith.

Christopher Ruff, S.T.L.

Acknowledgments

I would like gratefully to acknowledge the wonderful encouragement and support I have received from Bishop William P. Callahan in the undertaking of this project.

I would also like to thank Alice Andersen for her continued skilled editing and design.

Finally, and most of all, I would like to thank my wife Clare and my children, who have shown great patience with my late nights at the keyboard.

Christopher Ruff

Table of Contents

Introduction

The aim of these resources is to help Catholics at all levels of faith formation to discover more fully the profound beauty and personal relevance of the Catechism.

I start from the premise that every Catholic should be reading and re-reading this spiritual masterpiece —arguably the most profound articulation of our faith ever written. The Catechism belongs on the nightstand or the coffee table, not gathering dust on a reference shelf next to the dictionary. Its pages should be curled with use, like those (one would hope!) of the family Bible.

This is all the more true in this Year of Faith to which Pope Benedict XVI has called us, beginning Oct. 11, 2012. That date marks the 50th anniversary of the opening of the Second Vatican Council and the 20th anniversary of *Fidei Depositum* ("The Deposit of Faith"), by which Pope John Paul II ordered the Catechism to be published.

In *Fidei Depositum,* Blessed John Paul II wrote that the Catechism is "offered to all the faithful who wish to deepen their knowledge of the unfathomable riches of salvation" (n. 3). And Pope Benedict XVI is calling on Catholics during the Year of Faith to "rediscover and study...the *Catechism of the Catholic Church....* On page after page, we find that what is presented here is no theory, but an encounter with a Person who lives within the Church" (*Porta Fidei,* 11).

Unlocking a Treasure without Equal

It is an unfortunate reality that many Catholics find the Catechism intimidating. They often prefer to turn to simpler adaptations or to the *Compendium of the Catechism of the Catholic Church.* These are wonderful tools, but they simply cannot match the richness of the Catechism itself.

And so this series of study resources seeks to facilitate the reading experience of Catholics as they encounter the Catechism, providing solutions to the most common challenges it poses:

- Length – At nearly 700 pages (not counting the adjunct materials), the Catechism can intimidate by its sheer volume, and so the study resources are divided into manageable sessions, each covering about 15 pages of the Catechism.

- Density – Not only is the Catechism long, but virtually every paragraph is packed with meaning. That is its richness, but also its challenge. Even after reading a mere 10-20 pages, one can find oneself saying, "That was beautiful, but help me remember what I just read!" And so each study session offers a concise summary of the main points covered.

- Vocabulary – The Catechism makes full use of the Church's rich theological language. Again, that is both a blessing and a challenge.

Even if a Catholic has heard a particular expression many times—such as "Paschal Mystery"—he or she may have only a vague sense of its meaning. For that reason, each session contains a Vocabulary aid.

- Loftiness – The Catechism communicates with eloquent beauty the riches of the faith. And yet it must find its ultimate value in reaching down from the heights of theological discourse to the nitty-gritty of our daily lives. And so each session begins and ends with prayer and contains discussion questions and a "Growth in Discipleship" section that provoke personal reflection and application.

The summaries that form the main body of each session are brief and meant to be memory aids, capturing and commenting on a few principal themes. They could be compared to Internet maps that let the user zoom out from street level detail to high altitude "big picture." The summaries provide that big picture, helping the reader to keep his or her bearings in the midst of the rich but sometimes daunting detail of the Catechism.

But the map is meant only to make the trip easier, not to substitute for it. And so it is vital that participants prepare for each session by doing the assigned reading from the Catechism, which is really quite modest. It is there that they will experience the exquisite beauty of the journey through the Faith!

"The Faith of my Mother"

I would like to conclude these preliminary remarks with an excerpt from a book co-authored by Cardinal Christoph Schönborn, general editor of the Catechism, and then-Cardinal Joseph Ratzinger. At the conclusion of his section of the book, Cardinal Ratzinger writes that when the Catechism was in one of its final drafts before being published, it was shown to an elderly bishop known for his brilliant, scholarly mind. Ratzinger continues:

> He returned the manuscript with an expression of joy. Yes, he said, this is the faith of my mother. He rejoiced to find the faith which he had learned as a child and which had sustained him his whole life long expressed in its wealth and beauty, but also in its indestructible unity. This is the faith of my mother: the faith of our Mother, the Church. It is to this faith that the Catechism invites us. (*Introduction to the Catechism of the Catholic Church,* Ignatius Press, 1994, p. 36).

Let us now accept that invitation, embarking on a rich journey through this spiritual masterpiece, this gift from our Mother, the Church.

Christopher Ruff, S.T.L.

Keys to a Successful Catechism Study

Establishing Small Groups

- Recruit small group participants through personal invitation, parish announcements, bulletin inserts, etc. Spread the word to existing groups, such as bible study networks, parish committees, men's and women's organizations, young adults groups, etc. For resources, visit **www.novomill.com** and click on "Parish Launch Kit."

- For most people, once or twice a month is the most calendar-friendly meeting schedule, though weekly meetings can work well during Lent. Typical length for a session is about 90 minutes. Whatever time frame a group establishes, it should be rigorously respected.

- Each group needs a facilitator. It can be the same person at each meeting, or the facilitator role can rotate. The facilitator does not need expertise in the Catechism. His/her primary role is to start and end the meeting on time, to help keep things moving and on topic, and to foster a friendly, supportive environment in which everyone feels invited to contribute. Each facilitator will need to have a Facilitator's Guide.

- It is up to each group to decide where they would like to meet. It is ideal to hold the sessions in one another's homes since a key goal is to bring faith into daily life. If this is not workable, a room on church grounds is fine, or some combination of the two.

Acquiring the Necessary Resources

In addition to a copy of this study guide, *Unlocking the Beauty of the Catechism,* each participant will need to have:

- A copy of the *Catechism of the Catholic Church* —preferably the second edition, which reflects the changes made in 1997.

    ◊ I recommend the version published by the United States Conference of Catholic Bishops. It is green, and replaces the first edition, which was tan. It also includes appendices that available "compact" versions don't have, and its larger format features larger print. It is available in softcover only (the hardcover has been discontinued).

    ◊ If someone really wants a more compact version and is content not to have the appendices, a compact hardcover 2nd edition is published by Doubleday. This would be acceptable.

- A Catholic Bible.

    ◊ I recommend the Revised Standard Version, Catholic Edition, which is the version used in the Catechism itself and in this study guide. It is readily available from Ignatius Press.

◊ The second-best choice is the New American Bible, but any Catholic edition of the Bible is acceptable.

Preparing for the Sessions

In advance of each meeting, each participant is expected to:

1. First, read the material for the coming session from this study guide. It will summarize and highlight what to look for as you turn to the Catechism.

2. Then read the corresponding paragraphs of the Catechism itself, indicated on the session's title page (for example, for Session 2 read paragraphs 50-141).

3. Jot down answers to the discussion questions in the spaces provided, so as to come to the meeting prepared to share ideas.

Conducting the Session

1. The facilitator calls the gathering to order and all pray together the opening prayer.

2. The group participants then take turns reading aloud the study guide material for that session (one or two paragraphs at a time—whatever seems reasonable). This rotating pattern should continue through the discussion questions.

15

- **NOTE:** Consistent feedback has confirmed that this practice of reading aloud the study guide material enhances the group experience, even though participants have already read it on their own. Starting with the opening prayer, it typically takes only 10-15 minutes to arrive at the first discussion question.

3. If a discussion question asks for some passages of Scripture to be read, this should also be done aloud if time permits, though it is presumed that people have done this on their own in preparation for the meeting.

4. The facilitator has a Facilitator's Guide with "answer prompts" for some questions, and this may be helpful if the discussion stalls or there is confusion. But the guide should be used sparingly or it will get in the way of genuine discussion. The group should try to answer every question as thoroughly as possible before there is any consultation of the Facilitator's Guide.

5. If in the course of the discussion there arises a question or controversy that cannot be resolved in the group, the facilitator should consult the pastor or another resource person with a solid theological formation between sessions, bringing their response back to the group.

6. When there are 10-15 minutes left in the allotted schedule for the meeting, the facilitator should note that it is time to draw the discussion to a close (even if some discussion questions

remain) and to move on to reading the brief "Growth in Discipleship" section, and praying the "Group Prayers of Intercession."

7. The purpose of the "Growth in Discipleship" section is to provide ideas for personal application. These can be discussed if people wish, but there is no need for any commitments to be made publicly, unless people want to plan, for example, to pray the rosary together, or carry out some work of service, etc.

8. The "Group Prayers of Intercession" are intended to be spontaneous prayer intentions. They direct the power of prayer to various needs and simultaneously deepen the spirit of fellowship in the group. Conclude with the Lord's Prayer.

9. The session should end on time, even if members are eager to keep going. This is vital for the health and longevity of the group. The date and place of the next meeting should be confirmed.

10. It is good to follow the meeting with fifteen to twenty minutes of social time for those who are able to stay. Simple refreshments are a nice touch, with emphasis on the word simple. Otherwise people feel pressured to keep up with high expectations.

Group Etiquette

- Pray for the members of your group between sessions.

- Maintain confidentiality.

- Be a good listener and encourage everyone to contribute to the discussion, without anyone monopolizing. Members that are more talkative should allow everyone a chance to respond to a discussion question before they speak a second time.

- Love your neighbor by speaking charitably and refraining from any kind of gossip.

- Be on time, come prepared, and actively take part in discussion and prayer.

- Be open and expect God's action in your life and prayer—expect to be changed!

Unlocking the Beauty of The Catechism

The Creed: Part One

Session 1

A Symphony of the Faith

Reflection on
Introduction by
Pope John Paul II
and nn. 1-49

We reflect briefly on two key texts of Blessed Pope John Paul II, and then take our first step into the Catechism itself.

Opening Prayer

Come, Lord Jesus,
Bring the fire of your Spirit,
Who is light to our minds and warmth to our
hearts.
Help us to ponder and embrace the truth and
beauty of our Catholic Faith.
May the insights we gain be food for our souls,
Giving shape and meaning to our lives.

O Lord, as we begin this study we praise and
thank you for the great gift of the Catechism. We
thank you for our Mother the Church, guardian
and teacher of your truth, through whose hands
it has come to us. And we ask the intercession of
Blessed John Paul II, who shepherded this work of
faith from beginning to end. May the fruits of this
study make us stronger witnesses to you.
Amen.

Summary of Pope John Paul II's Words of Promulgation

The Pope Who Brought us the Catechism

It is fitting that we begin this study of the *Catechism of the Catholic Church* by summarizing very briefly two documents of Blessed Pope John Paul II by which he authoritatively announced the two stages of its publication. These very short papal documents are at the beginning of the book.

Laetamur Magnopere ("We Rejoice Greatly")

"A cause for great joy." That is how Blessed Pope John Paul II characterizes the completion in 1997 of the official Latin edition of the *Catechism of the Catholic Church,* in his Apostolic Letter approving and promulgating it, *Laetamur Magnopere.*

The Catechism had first been published in French in 1992. But now, with the appearance of the Latin "Typical Edition" incorporating a variety of modest revisions, the French—like every other language edition—had to be modified to conform to it. This was in keeping with the general Church practice of publishing the authoritative versions of Vatican documents in Latin.

In his letter, Pope John Paul II expresses deep satisfaction in this Catechism and its "genuine, systematic presentation of the faith." He refers to it as a "sure norm" for teaching and expresses the wish that it be "known and shared by everyone," playing a significant role in the new evangelization.

Fidei Depositum ("Deposit of Faith")

From *Laetamur Magnopere* we turn—forward in the book, but backward in time—to the Apostolic Constitution *Fidei Depositum,* by which Pope John Paul II first authorized the publication of the Catechism in 1992, on the 30th anniversary of the opening of the Second Vatican Council. He describes the Catechism as a fruit of Vatican II, whose chief purpose was to find a way suited to our times to express all the strength and beauty of the Faith.

Pope John Paul II goes on to trace its roots still farther back, noting that its four-part structure mirrors the structure of the 16th century Catechism of the Council of Trent. And so while this Catechism is fresh and new in its mode of expression, it evidences the profound unity of the Church's faith across space and time. It also reflects the collaboration of the bishops of the whole world, who had extensive input into its composition. Thanks to these many voices of collaboration, Pope John Paul II refers to the Catechism as a "symphony of the faith."

Summary of nn. 1-49

Prologue

The Life of Man—To Know and Love God

"FATHER,...this is eternal life, that they may know you, the only true God, and Jesus Christ whom you have sent" (Jn 17:3).

These are the very first words of the Catechism, words taken directly from Scripture and centered on the *personal relationship* God calls us to have with him. Continuing this emphasis, the opening paragraph begins:

> God, infinitely perfect and blessed in himself, in a plan of sheer goodness freely created man to make him share in his own blessed life. For this reason, at every time and in every place, God draws close to man. He calls man to seek him, to know him, to love him with all his strength (n. 1).

Two dominant threads of the Catechism are thus evident right away. First, Sacred Scripture will be its heart and soul. In the words of then-Cardinal Joseph Ratzinger (now Pope Benedict XVI), the Catechism is "shaped from one end to the other by the Bible. As far as I know, there has never been until now a catechism so thoroughly formed by the Bible" *(Gospel, Catechesis, Catechism,* Ignatius Press, 1997, p. 61).

The second dominant thread is the Catechism's *personal, relational* approach. Though any catechism is by its nature a teaching instrument, the Catechism of the Catholic Church is at bottom a love story! It lives and breathes the mystical joy of the great saints it so often quotes: Thérèse of Lisieux, John of the Cross, Irenaeus, Teresa of Avila, and so many others.

It is interesting that the most frequently quoted saint is not the person one might expect for a catechism. It is not St. Thomas Aquinas, who we might call the premiere "theologian of the intellect." To be fair, he is the second most quoted, and rightly so. But the most oft-quoted saint is St. Augustine, the passionate "theologian of the heart" so well known for the deeply personal conversion he describes in his *Confessions.* His most famous saying is, "You have made us for yourself, O Lord, and our heart is restless until it rests in you" *(Confessions* 1,1).

This is the spirit of the Catechism, which beautifully balances the need to *communicate the Catholic Faith with clarity*—drawing not just on the Bible and the saints, but on a whole array of Popes and Councils and documents—with the need to *show forth the radiant, loving face of Christ.*

Catechesis and the Use of the Catechism

All of us are called to be disciples of Christ and to hand on, from one generation to the next, the gift of faith we have received. This vital process of teaching the Faith is called catechesis, and it is discussed in nn. 4-10 of the Catechism.

In nn. 11-24 we see a description of the aim and structure of the Catechism, which is divided into four parts or "pillars" that focus on creed, sacraments, moral life and prayer.

The Catechism is first of all a point of reference for the bishops of the world, as they teach the Faith to their flocks. But it is also meant to help and inspire catechists (religion teachers of all kinds), and indeed all the faithful.

The Catechism's layout and system of references is covered briefly in nn. 18-22. Read these few paragraphs attentively and flip through the pages of the Catechism to become acquainted with what is being described. Note especially the appendices at the back of the book.

The Prologue ends in n. 25 with a beautiful quote from the 16th century *Roman Catechism* (the Catechism of the Council of Trent), which puts a final "exclamation point" on the whole purpose of Church doctrine and teaching— love.

The Profession of Faith

With the introductory portions completed, we now begin in earnest our study of the first pillar of the Catechism—the Creed, the Profession of Faith.

Man's Capacity for God

In nn. 27-49, the Catechism considers our built-in capacity for God and the ways we may come to know and speak about him. Read this section prayerfully, entering into its spirit, as what follows is only a quick sketch.

God created us to seek, to know and to love him, and that explains mankind's religious expressions and yearnings throughout history. But this built-in desire for God can be clouded unless we live with an upright heart.

It is possible for us to come to know at least the existence of God even without God's revelation. We can do this by reflecting on the nature, order and beauty of the world, as well as the nature and qualities of the human person. But to know and love God in a deeper and more intimate way, we need his revelation and grace. This is so especially because original sin has left us with weakened minds and wills and disordered desires. As a result, we are easily tempted to distort the truth and to rationalize wrong choices, closing our eyes to truths that challenge us to conversion.

Human language can speak truths about God because we can see him reflected in what he has created. But even those truths are far from the full reality of God, because our limited human words and concepts can never contain him.

Next session we will consider in greater depth God's Revelation, especially through Sacred Scripture and Sacred Tradition.

Vocabulary

Typical Edition *(Laetamur Magnopere,* opening line) –
From two Latin roots: *typus,* for "model" or "pattern," and
editio, for "a bringing forth," a "production." So in pronounc-
ing the 1997 Latin edition the editio typica, or "Typical
Edition," the Pope is declaring it to be the authoritative
model or standard against which all other versions are to be
measured.

Promulgated (LM, second sentence) – From the Latin
pro, meaning "for," and *vulgare* or *vulgus,* referring to "the
people," "the public." In Church language then, this means
that a document or a law is put forth publicly, declared and
enacted.

Catechism (LM, paragraph 8) – From the Greek *katekhein,*
which means "to resound" (see n. 2) or "to echo." To engage
in catechesis is to echo faithfully God's Word, to echo the
Gospel, to echo the faith of the Church. And of course that is
the whole purpose of the Catechism.

Liturgy *(Depositum Fidei,* paragraph 8) – From the Greek
leitourgia, for "work of the people," it refers to the official,
public worship of the Church, which includes the Mass, the
Sacraments, the Liturgy of the Hours or Breviary, and sacra-
mentals (such as blessings or the use of holy water).

Canon Law (DF, paragraph 8) – From the Greek *kanon,*
for a reed or stick used for measuring, it refers here to the
Church's body of laws that regulate her members and their
responsibilities. As a side note, recall that the Church "can-
onizes" saints, meaning she measures their heroic virtue and
then declares them to be in heaven and thus to be a measuring stick for our lives.

Exegetes (DF, 1) – From the Greek *exegesis,* meaning "to
lead out." Here it refers to Scripture scholars who draw out

or interpret the meaning of biblical texts.

Episcopate (DF, 1) – From the Greek *episkopos,* for "overseer," used already in the New Testament to refer to a bishop (cf., 1 Timothy 3:1-7). Episcopate refers to all the bishops of the world, as a group.

Magisterium (DF, 2) – From the Latin *magister,* for "teacher," it refers to the teaching authority of the Church, which belongs to the Pope and the bishops in communion with him.

Ecclesial (DF, 3) – From the Latin *ecclesia,* for "church." "Ecclesial" thus is an adjective; so "ecclesial communion" means communion (unity, harmony) of the Church.

Apostolic See (DF, 3) – The word "see" comes from the Latin *sedem,* for a "seat." A "see" is a diocese and refers to the district under the jurisdiction of a bishop. The Apostolic See is the diocese of Rome, under the jurisdiction of the Pope. To be in communion with the Apostolic See means to be in unity, agreement, with the Pope.

Fathers of the Church (8) – Theologians of the first eight centuries who were eminent in holiness and learning (for example, St. Jerome, St. Augustine, St. John Chrysostom), and who had a special role in articulating the Faith.

Apologetic (20) – From the Greek *apologia,* for "defense." Apologetic observations would be remarks that defend or explain certain Catholic beliefs or practices.

Patristic (21) – From the Latin word *pater,* meaning "father," patristic observations would be those which are rooted in the writings of the Fathers of the Church (see above).

Hagiographical (22) – From the Greek *hagios,* for "holy" and *graphia,* for "writing." Hagiographical observations would be writings of, or about, the saints, the holy men and women of the Church down through the centuries.

31

Discussion Questions

1. Some of us grew up with the Baltimore Catechism, which had its roots in the *Catechism of the Council of Trent* from the 16th century (the only other universal catechism in the history of the Church). Both the Baltimore Catechism and the *Catechism of the Catholic Church* contain the same fundamental truths, but the manner of expression is different.

   From the little you have seen so far of this Catechism, how would you characterize the difference, if you remember the Baltimore Catechism (if you are too young, search for it on the Internet and have a look)? Why do you suppose many say the manner of expression of this Catechism is more suited to the times in which we live?

   _____

   _____

   _____

   _____

   _____

   _____

2. In *Fidei Depositum,* the Pope writes that on every level the Church is "called to a new effort of evangelization." And the Catechism states: "Those who with God's help have welcomed Christ's call and freely responded to it are urged on by love of Christ to proclaim the Good News everywhere in the world" (n. 3). Yet Catholic lay people very often seem to be shy about evangelizing others, calling them to Christ and to faith. Why do you suppose this is? If we were less shy about it, what would we be doing, what *should* we be doing, day to day?

---

3. The Prologue to the Catechism ends with a beautiful quote from the *Catechism of the Council of Trent:*

> "The whole concern of doctrine and its teaching must be directed to the love that never ends. Whether something is proposed for belief, for hope or for action, the love of our Lord must always be made accessible, so that anyone can see that all the works of perfect Christian virtue spring from love and have no other objective than to arrive at love."

What is the essential message here, and the importance of that message?

_____

_____

_____

_____

_____

_____

4. Have someone read n. 27. Is the desire for God written in your heart? How do you know? How does it manifest itself?

_____

_____

_____

_____

_____

_____

5. Number 29 lists a number of factors that can bring man to forget, overlook, or even explicitly reject his bond with God. Have you seen some of these factors at work in the world and even in yourself at times? Discuss.

_____

_____

_____

_____

_____

_____

_____

_____

6. Read the quote from Pope Pius XII in n. 37. Is the point he is making evident in society today—indeed, even in our own lives at times? Discuss.

_____

_____

_____

_____

_____

_____

7. Numbers 31-35 and 41 note that all creation reflects
    God in some way, especially man, so that "from
    the greatness and beauty of created things comes a
    corresponding perception of their Creator" (Wisdom
    13:5).

    What realities or characteristics in the human
    person and in the natural world draw you closer to
    an awareness of God? Can you think of a time when
    God became quite real and close to you because of
    something you saw in another person or in nature?

    _____

    _____

    _____

    _____

    _____

    _____

    _____

Growth in Discipleship

Possible ways to put the themes of this session into action:

- Taking time regularly with one's children (or others in one's care) to teach/discuss the Faith
- Offering and training to be a catechist in one's parish
- Making a point to contemplate God in the beauty of creation
- Finding ways to witness to that love of God which is the purpose and goal of all Church doctrine

Group Prayers of Intercession

8 to 10 Minutes — Conclude with the Lord's Prayer.

Session 2

God Comes to Meet Us

Reflection on
nn. 50-141

*We reflect on the manner in which God has
revealed himself to us, particularly through
Sacred Scripture and Tradition, faithfully
handed on by the Church.*

Opening Prayer

Come, Lord Jesus,

Bring the fire of your Spirit,

Who is light to our minds and warmth to our
hearts.

Help us to ponder and embrace the truth and
beauty of our Catholic Faith.

May the insights we gain be food for our souls,

Giving shape and meaning to our lives.

Heavenly Father, we praise and thank you for
revealing yourself to us, that we might know you
and share your very life. We thank you for the gift
of your only Son, Jesus Christ, in whose face we
behold your face. We thank you for your inspired
word in the Holy Scriptures, by which we are
taught and nourished. We thank you for the gift
of the Church that, led by the Holy Spirit, guards
and professes the faith that lights the path to our
salvation. May our minds and hearts be ever open,
and our wills humbly obedient, to the truths she
proclaims in your name.

Amen.

Summary of nn. 50-141

Article 1 – The Revelation of God

God has willed from the beginning that we know him, love him and become sharers in his divine life. Over time, he has revealed himself to us in stages, by both words and actions.

In nn. 54-64, in a concise but beautiful way, the story of God's dealings with man is told, from Adam and Eve through Noah, Abraham and the Chosen People of Israel, finally reaching its culmination in and through Jesus Christ. The Catechism's telling of this story is incredibly rich and should be read slowly and prayerfully. It is an epic marked by sin and redemption, with covenant following covenant. Called by God to be his People, Israel has a central but not exclusive place in this story.

From the Chosen People comes the Messiah, Christ our Redeemer, from whom the full Revelation of God shines out to all mankind. As Jesus will later tell the Apostle Philip, "he who has seen me has seen the Father" (Jn 14:9). Christ and his words and deeds are God's final "public revelation," safeguarded, pondered and faithfully handed on by his Church.

Article 2 – The Transmission of Divine Revelation

God "desires all men to be saved and to come to the knowledge of the truth" (1 Timothy 2:4).

Jesus, "the Way, the Truth and the Life" (cf., John 14:6), is God's ultimate Revelation through his teachings, his deeds, and his very being. In nn. 75-79, the Catechism recalls that Jesus commanded the apostles to hand on his Gospel, his Revelation. They did so in two fundamental ways:

- *Orally* and through their actions and decisions. This "living transmission" (n. 78) is called Tradition;
- *In writing,* through the Sacred Scriptures.

In order that this Revelation would be faithfully preserved, the apostles left bishops as their successors in shepherding the Church. Jesus promised the Holy Spirit would always be with and guide his Church.

As noted in nn. 80-83, Sacred Scripture and Sacred Tradition are inseparable. In fact, one could say that Sacred Scripture *flows out of* Sacred Tradition.

In nn. 84-90, the Catechism helps us see that divine Revelation—the "deposit of the faith" handed on through Sacred Scripture and Sacred Tradition—must have a guaranteed, faithful interpreter through the ages. Otherwise we would easily lose our way amid thousands of conflicting interpretations on crucial matters of faith and morals.

Jesus has protected us from such confusion by establishing a Church led by the apostles and their successors, of whom Jesus said, "He who hears you, hears me" (Luke 10:16). This is the Magisterium, constituted by the Successor of Peter, the Pope, and the Bishops in communion with him. The Magisterium defines and explains Church doctrine, including dogmas and other definitive teachings, thus illuminating our life of faith, our path to Christ. Church doctrine always has its roots in divine Revelation.

The Holy Spirit graces the faithful followers of Christ and his Church with a sense of the faith *(sensus fidei)*, a kind of spiritual instinct by which they understand, embrace and apply the faith more deeply in their lives, under the guidance of the Magisterium.

Article 3 – Sacred Scripture

The Sacred Scriptures are the inspired word of God, nourishing and strengthening the Church. All the Scriptures center on and point to Christ as their fulfillment.

In nn. 106-107, we read that all that the inspired authors of Sacred Scripture affirm "should be regarded as affirmed by the Holy Spirit" (Vatican II's *Dei Verbum,* 11). We face a mystery here, in that the sacred authors employed their own styles and skills as true authors, and yet God inspired them in such a way that they wrote "whatever he wanted written, and no more" *(ibid.).*

In order to interpret Scripture correctly, we must strive to understand *both* what the human author intended to say *and* what God intends to say through them (which may be more than the human author realized at the time he wrote). The Catechism gives us the principles necessary to approach this interpretation faithfully (note the three criteria for interpretation in nn. 112-114, and the two senses of Scripture in nn. 115-118). The ultimate authority in matters of interpretation is the Church.

It is also important to note, as pointed out in n. 120, that it is only through the Church's Tradition that we know which writings belong in the list (or canon) of sacred books making up Sacred Scripture. There were a significant number of "contenders" (such as the *Gospel of Thomas*, the *Gospel of Peter,* and the *Third Letter to the Corinthians)* which were ruled by the early Church to be inauthentic and not inspired. This could not have been "sorted out" without the authority of Tradition, guided by the Holy Spirit.

The Church accepts the writings of both the Old and the New Testament as inspired, though the Old Testament contains "matters imperfect and provisional" *(Dei Verbum,* 15) and finds its ultimate fulfillment in the New Testament, centered on Christ and the Gospels (see the discussion of typology in nn. 128-130).

The Sacred Scriptures are central to the life of the Church—"strength for the faith and food for the soul" *(Dei Verbum,* 21). They are essential sources for preaching, teaching, meditation and growth in holiness.

Next session we will consider our proper response to God who has revealed himself.

Vocabulary

Apostolic (75) – Of or pertaining to the Apostles; coming down to us from the Apostles.

Canonical (105) – As noted in Session 1, this comes from the Greek *kanon,* for a reed or stick used for measuring. It refers here to that which has been measured or ruled as belonging to the official list of sacred books (see 120).

Divine economy (56) – From the Greek *oikos,* or "household," and *nomia,* or "management," this refers to the way God "manages" the world, the way he unfolds his plan of salvation for mankind.

Exegesis (116) – See Vocabulary for Session 1.

Local church (83) – The Church as it exists in a particular place, a particular diocese. By its nature, every local church remains organically united with the universal Church, the whole Church.

Patriarchs (60) – The leaders of the Israelite tribes and heads of prominent families who appear in Genesis from Adam to Joseph. Especially significant are Abraham, Isaac and Jacob.

Pedagogy (122) – The art of teaching step by step.

Polytheism (57) – From Greek *polus,* for "many," and *theos,* for "god," thus belief in many gods.

Sensus Fidelium (67) – Latin, meaning the "sense of the faithful." Refers to the God-given instinct that the Church's faithful have for discerning the true from the false.

Typology (128) – The discovery in Old Testament persons and events of foreshadowings or "types" of persons and events that occur in the New Covenant of Christ. For example, Moses as lawgiver on Mount Sinai is a type (or foreshadowing) of Christ as lawgiver in his Sermon on the Mount.

Discussion Questions

1. The Catechism teaches that Jesus is the fulfillment of all God's Revelation, the final and unsurpassable Word. What attributes of God do you see revealed in the life of Christ? Point to some incidents in the Gospels that illustrate those attributes.

---

2. Discuss the difference between public Revelation and private revelations (see nn. 66-67). What are some examples of private revelations that have been approved by the Church?

_____

_____

_____

_____

_____

_____

_____

_____

3. Each of us is indebted to certain people who in the course of our lives were instrumental in encouraging and forming our faith. Who has affected your life in this way, and how?

_____

_____

_____

_____

_____

_____

_____

4. We read in n. 79 that the "...Father's self-communication, made through his Word in the Holy Spirit, remains present and active in the Church: 'God, who spoke in the past, continues to converse with the Spouse of his beloved Son' *(Dei Verbum,* 8)."

In other words, God continues to act in the Church and to communicate himself through her.

It is obvious in today's world that there is a crisis of faith on precisely this point. Many (including many Catholics) do not believe Christ's words, "He who hears you, hears me" (Luke 10:16), with reference to the Church.

- What influences have fostered this doubt?

- What can we do to help preserve in ourselves and our loved ones a vibrant faith that to hear the Church is to hear Christ?

_____

_____

_____

_____

_____

_____

5. Define each of the following and describe how they are related to one another:

    a) Scripture;
    b) Tradition;
    c) Magisterium.

_____

_____

_____

_____

_____

_____

_____

_____

_____

6. Read together nn. 91-93 of the Catechism, with regard to the *sensus fidei*. How can we understand this in light of the fact that substantial numbers of people who call themselves Catholic actively disagree with the Magisterium (Pope and bishops) on key teachings, especially in the area of morality?

_____

_____

_____

_____

_____

_____

7. Numbers 115-119 of the Catechism discuss two fundamental meanings of Scripture: the literal sense and the spiritual sense.

    Read Exodus 12:1-13. What is this "literally" about? What is its spiritual sense (specifically "allegorical" —see n. 117 of the Catechism)? It may help you also to read John 1:29, Luke 22:14-20 and Revelation 5:6-14 to get the full impact of the spiritual/allegorical sense.

    _____

    _____

    _____

    _____

    _____

    _____

8. In discussing the unique place of the four Gospels in the Church's life, the Catechism quotes St. Therese of Lisieux:

> "But above all it's the Gospels that occupy my mind when I'm at prayer; my poor soul has so many needs, and yet this is the one thing needful. I'm always finding fresh lights there, hidden and enthralling meanings" (*Autobiography,* Manuscript A).

- What parts of the Bible have spoken to you most profoundly?

- Do you have a favorite Gospel or Gospel passage?

- What helps you or hinders you in making the Bible a significant part of your life of personal prayer and devotion?

Growth in Discipleship

Possible ways to put the themes of this session into action:

- Daily reading and praying with Scripture
- Praying for someone's heart to be opened to faith
- Praying for the Pope and the bishops as they proclaim with authority the truths of our Catholic Faith

Group Prayers of Intercession

8 to 10 Minutes – Conclude with the Lord's Prayer.

Session 3

Our Response of Faith

Reflection on
nn. 142-197

We reflect on our proper response, stirred by the Holy Spirit, to God who has revealed himself.

Opening Prayer

Come, Lord Jesus,
Bring the fire of your Spirit,
Who is light to our minds and warmth to our
  hearts.
Help us to ponder and embrace the truth and
  beauty of our Catholic Faith.
May the insights we gain be food for our souls,
Giving shape and meaning to our lives.

O Lord, you have let your face shine upon us,[1]
And spoken to us by your Word.[2]
May we respond gratefully with the faith of Abra-
ham, the faith of Mary,
Believing all that you have revealed,
And entrusting ourselves personally and totally to
you.

And when challenges befall us and the path ahead
is unclear,
May we always echo, by your grace, the words of
St. Peter:
"Lord, to whom shall we go? You have the words of
eternal life."[3]

Amen.

---

[1]Cf., Num 6:25; Ps 119:135
[2]Cf., Heb 1:1-2
[3]Jn 6:68

Summary of nn. 142-197

Article 1 – I Believe

In two short paragraphs worthy of profound meditation, the Catechism introduces faith as rooted in an extraordinary *relationship:*

- "God, from the fullness of his love, addresses men as his friends, and moves among them, in order to invite and receive them into his own company" (n. 142, quoting *Dei Verbum* 2).

- *"By faith,* man completely submits his intellect and his will to God. With his whole being man gives his assent to God the revealer" (n. 143).

The Catechism next holds up two pillars of faith: Abraham from the Old Testament, the model of faithful submission to God, and Mary from the New Testament, who is its "most perfect embodiment" (n. 144), and whose faith never wavered, even at the foot of the cross.

In nn. 150-152 we read that faith is adherence both *to God himself* and *to the truths he has revealed.* In faith we place absolute belief and trust in God. The Son reveals the Father, and the Holy Spirit reveals to us the Son, enabling us to say, "Jesus is Lord" (cf., 1 Cor 12:3).

The Catechism lays out the characteristics of faith in nn. 153-165. First of all, faith is both a *gift of grace* (we can't achieve or earn it on our own) and a truly *human act of cooperation* with that grace (we don't just sit back passively). Another characteristic of faith is that even though it goes beyond the power of reason, it certainly is not irrational (clear and reasonable thinking and science support it). We can also say of faith that it must be *free,* not forced, that it is *necessary* for salvation, that it *can be lost* if it is not nurtured, and that in a dim and partial way *it gives us a foretaste of eternal life.*

Article 2 – We Believe

In nn. 166-175, the Catechism notes that faith does not come to us in isolation. We have been blessed to receive it in community, nurtured by other people. Love of God and neighbor summons us in turn to share this treasure with others.

The Church is our mother in the life of faith, safeguarding it and passing on its truths, so that in every place and time the Faith is one and the same, constant and reliable, even if expressed in different languages (read slowly the beautiful quote from St. Irenaeus in n. 173).

The Profession of the Christian Faith

The Creeds

As the Catechism notes in n. 186, the Church from the beginning wished to summarize the central articles of the Faith, especially so these could be professed by candidates for baptism. A number of professions of the one Catholic Faith were formulated at different times and places, but two stand out: the Apostles' Creed and the Nicene Creed. The Apostles' Creed is the more ancient of the two, rooted in the early Church in Rome. It is professed at baptisms, either by the candidate or, in the case of infant baptism, by the parents. It is also customarily recited at the beginning of the Rosary. The Nicene (or Niceno-Constantinopolitan) Creed, drawn from the fourth century Councils of Nicaea and Constantinople, is the longer of the two and is professed at Sunday Mass.

In its commentary, the Catechism follows the format of the Apostles' Creed, with occasional references to the Nicene Creed. The two creeds are printed side by side in the transition pages between n. 184 and n. 185 of the Catechism.

Next session we will consider the mystery of God as a Trinity of Persons.

Vocabulary

Supernatural virtue, infused (153) – From Latin *super,* meaning "above," and *natura,* meaning "nature." Faith is not a natural virtue, like human courage, that we can stir up inside ourselves by our own efforts. Rather, it is a supernatural virtue which must be infused in us, poured into us, from God above.

Beatific vision (163) – From Latin *beatus,* for "blessed" or "happy." The beatific vision is the unending, blissful "face-to-face" vision of God enjoyed by all who attain heaven.

Discussion Questions

1. The Catechism tells us that faith is a gift of God and that man's heart must be stirred and converted by the Holy Spirit, "who opens the eyes of the mind and 'makes it easy for all to accept and believe the truth'" (n. 153). But the Catechism adds that God has wished to aid our faith by providing *external proofs* of his Revelation, including "the miracles of Christ and the saints, prophecies, the Church's growth and holiness, and her fruitfulness and stability" (n. 156).

   - Which of these "external proofs" of God's Revelation have bolstered your faith?
   - Are there any other external supports that have helped you?

_____

_____

_____

_____

_____

_____

_____

_____

2. The Catechism in n. 158 quotes a famous saying of St. Augustine: "I believe, in order to understand; and I understand, the better to believe" *(Sermo 43,7,9)*. What do you think he meant by this rather mysterious phrase?

_____

_____

_____

_____

_____

_____

3. We read in n. 161 that belief in Jesus Christ and
    in the One who sent him is necessary for salva-
    tion. What about those who—especially in the past,
    but even today—have never heard of Christ? Look
    ahead to nn. 846-848 and discuss.

    _____

    _____

    _____

    _____

    _____

    _____

4. In n. 162, the Catechism connects certain conditions with either perseverance in, or the loss of, the gift of faith. Discuss one by one these conditions and the relevance you think each has to faith.

_____

_____

_____

_____

_____

_____

_____

5. The Catechism is not naive about the challenge of faith, quoting St. Paul's words in n. 164, that we perceive God as "in a mirror, dimly" and only "in part" (1 Cor 13:12). It notes that faith is often tested by the world we live in, by the realities of evil, suffering, injustice and death. These can shake us and tempt us to lose faith.

   • What do you see as the greatest challenges to faith? What has helped you to deal with them?

   • Why do you suppose God has not made everything crystal clear and easy? Read 1 Peter 1:3-9 for insight.

_____

_____

_____

_____

_____

_____

_____

6. In n. 166, the Catechism makes a beautiful statement about the community dimension of faith, about our interconnectedness and reliance on one another. Read it together now. Do you sense the truth of this statement? When and how has it become real for you?

_____

_____

_____

_____

_____

_____

_____

7. Some would say that in today's world many people
    have a reawakened hunger for faith, for certain-
    ties, for sure moral teaching, and that the Catholic
    Church stands out for not having compromised and
    watered down her teachings. Discuss.

_____

_____

_____

_____

_____

_____

8. Pray (slowly and deliberately) the Nicene Creed together as written following n. 184. We pray it every Sunday at Mass and it links us with nearly 1700 years of Christian faith and worship. Take a moment silently to reflect on the millions of voices that have proclaimed and even died for that faith.

Growth in Discipleship

Possible ways to put the themes of this session into action:

- Meditating on Hebrews 11 (tribute to faith)
- Praying for an increase in your faith
- Praying for someone else to come to faith
- Daily praying of the Apostles' or Nicene Creed
- Discussing with family or friends after Sunday Mass the power and beauty of the Creed we profess together

Group Prayers of Intercession

8 to 10 Minutes – Conclude with the Lord's Prayer.

Session 4

The God in Whom We Believe

Reflection on
nn. 198-267

We continue to reflect on the first line of the Apostles' Creed: "I believe in God, the Father Almighty, Creator of Heaven and Earth," focusing on the central mystery of Three Persons in One God.

Opening Prayer

Come, Lord Jesus,

Bring the fire of your Spirit,

Who is light to our minds and warmth to our
hearts.

Help us to ponder and embrace the truth and
beauty of our Catholic Faith.

May the insights we gain be food for our souls,

Giving shape and meaning to our lives.

How patient you have been with us, O Lord,
leading us by the hand from Old Covenant to New,
revealing your glory bit by bit. It is still too much
for our mortal minds, but we believe you, we adore
you, we place our trust in you—Father, Son and
Holy Spirit.

Amen.

Summary of nn. 198-267

Article 1 – "I Believe in God the Father Almighty, Creator of Heaven and Earth"

We begin with the first line of the Creed, "I believe in God the Father almighty, creator of heaven and earth." In fact, the Catechism will be discussing this opening statement of faith for many pages (nn. 199-421).

Paragraph 1 – I Believe in God

In nn. 198-231 the Catechism reflects on our belief in *one* God, and how that truth was revealed to the Israelites in the Old Testament and later confirmed by Jesus (but with the surprising twist that the one God was also three persons).

Note the beautiful reflection in nn. 203-213 on what it means that God revealed to us his "name." We see that he is living and eternal, constant in mercy and love, trustworthy and true. Sin enters the world when the devil ("a liar and the father of lies"—John 8:44) tempts man to doubt God's truthfulness and love, presenting him instead as a rival trying to oppress man and hold him back.

Read with prayerful attention "the implications of faith in One God" in nn. 222-227.

Paragraph 2 – The Father

The rest of this session (nn. 232-267) deals with our belief in God as a Trinity of Persons in one God, which is "the central mystery of Christian faith and life" (n. 234). This truth was unknown in Old Testament times. It took Jesus to reveal that there was not only a loving and all-powerful Father, but a Son and a Holy Spirit as well. No mystery of our faith is more difficult to grasp than the reality of one God in three persons. Even the greatest theologians and mystics have humbly acknowledged the inadequacy of the human mind to contain it. Patience, humility and prayer are needed here, as this is perhaps the most difficult section of the Catechism!

Note that nn. 245-248 deal with a somewhat complex question about the Holy Spirit, who "proceeds (comes forth) from the Father and the Son." It has to do with an ancient controversy between the Catholic Church and the Eastern Orthodox churches. The teaching of the Catholic Church on this matter can be found perhaps more plainly summarized in nn. 263 and 264.

What follow are some key points in the overall discussion of the Trinity:

- God is one God, but in that one God are three distinct persons. Of course, we human beings are distinct persons too, but that is because we are separate beings. God is not three separate Gods, but one.

- The three persons in God—Father, Son, and Holy Spirit—are equally eternal and equally divine, having one substance, one nature. Their distinction is in their *relationship* to each other. The Father *generates* the Son from all eternity and the Holy Spirit *proceeds* from the Father and the Son from all eternity. It is critical to understand that it is not a question of "first the Father, then the Son, then the Holy Spirit." Everything is simultaneous and eternal in God. He exists outside time.

- In nn. 257-260, the Catechism stresses that the whole work of creation, revelation and redemption, the whole divine "economy" or governance of the world, is one common work of the three divine persons. For example, though we often tend to attribute creation to the Father, all three persons accomplished the creation as one God. Still, as noted in n. 258, "each divine person performs the common work according to his unique personal property." This is especially evident in the Incarnation of the Son and the gift of the Holy Spirit.

- "[T]he whole Christian life is a communion with each of the divine persons, without in any way separating them. Everyone who glorifies the Father does so through the Son and in the Holy Spirit; everyone who follows Christ does so because the Father draws him and the Spirit moves him" (n. 259). Ultimately, we are called by God to be united with him in his very life, the life of the Trinity. As the lives of many saints attest, this union can begin even now, but it will culminate in heaven.

When all is said and done, there is incredible beauty in the doctrine of the Trinity, for it reveals to us that God's life is not that of a solitary being, but of a deep, interpersonal communion of love. We would never have guessed that, had God himself not revealed it to us.

Next session we will consider the wonder of God's creation.

Vocabulary

Theophany (204) – From Greek *theos* for "God," and *phain-ein*, "to show," it refers to God's act of manifesting himself, showing himself, as to Moses at the burning bush in Exodus 3.

YHWH (206) – YHWH represents the Hebrew letters "Yod-Heh-Waw-Heh," and is the ancient name God revealed to Moses as recorded in Exodus 3:15. Its pronunciation is uncertain, but is likely "Yahweh." Most scholars think it comes from a Hebrew verb which means "to be" or "to exist." This would make it a repetition or echo of what God has just said to Moses in the previous verse: "I AM WHO I AM," and "I AM" (Ex 3:14). Jewish reverence for God's name is such that it is not pronounced when the Scriptures are read, but is replaced by the divine title "LORD" (cf., n. 209).

Ineffable (206) – Unable to be put into words, utterly mysterious.

Hierarchy of the truths of faith (234) – Our faith teaches many truths, but some are more central or primary, forming the foundation for others. The Trinity is such a truth, as are the Divinity of Christ and his redeeming death and Resurrection. Others, such as the perpetual virginity of Mary, are no less true, but their truth and significance correlate with and refer back to the more primary truths (Mary was perpetually a virgin because of the uniquely divine and human Son she was called to bear).

Deity (238) – From Latin *Deus,* deity means God, or having the status of God.

Transcendent authority (239) – From Latin *trans* for "across" or "beyond," and *scandere,* "to climb." To transcend is thus to "rise beyond." God is on a completely different level from the world he has created, a world which he rules with absolute power, wisdom and love.

God's immanence (239) – From Latin *in,* the same as English "in," and *manere,* or "to remain," immanence means a "remaining within," a "dwelling within." Even though God is on a completely different level from the world, he is at the same time intimately present to that world. Indeed, he has entered that world and taken on flesh in Christ.

Consubstantial (242) – From Latin *con,* for "with," and *substantia,* for "substance," consubstantial means sharing the same substance.

Spiration (246) – From Latin *spirare,* "to breathe," thus the "breathing forth" of the Holy Spirit, by the Father and the Son. Recall that the Risen Christ "breathes" the Spirit on the apostles in John 20:22.

Triune (254) – From Latin *tres,* for "three," and *unus,* for "one," triune means "three-in-one."

Discussion Questions

1. Why do you suppose God, in his revelation to the Israelites, focused so intently on his being *one* God and did not communicate the truth that he is also three persons?"

_____

_____

_____

_____

_____

_____

2. In n. 206, the Catechism says that in telling Moses
    he was YHWH (Yahweh), God in one sense revealed
    a name, but in another sense *refused* to accept a
    name.

    •   Read the paragraph in question and discuss
        what you think the Catechism means by this.

    •   Mention two or three other insights that
        made an impression on you from this section
        on the significance of God's "name" (nn. 203-
        213).

---

3. Number 208 states, "Faced with God's fascinating and mysterious presence, man discovers his own insignificance." The Catechism then gives examples from the Bible in which men such as Isaiah in the Old Testament and Peter in the New Testament shrink from God's awesome presence out of a sense of their own unworthiness.

- Do you think we have sometimes lost a sense of this "fear of the Lord" in recent decades, and if so, why?

- Might it have been a reaction to something else?

_____

_____

_____

_____

_____

_____

4. Read Jesus' dialogue with the Jews in the Gospel of John 8:39-59. Discuss the profound significance of Jesus' choice of words in verse 58 (see n. 211).

_____

_____

_____

_____

_____

_____

5. Read the beautiful prayer of St. Teresa of Jesus in n. 227.

   • What difference do you think a prayer like that might make if you started and ended your day with it?

   • If there are any particular prayers that inspire and strengthen your faith, mention them and discuss why.

   _____

   _____

   _____

   _____

   _____

   _____

6. The main points of the Church's doctrine on the Trinity are discussed in the Catechism (nn. 232-267) and in the commentary for this session.

   • In reading about this great and central mystery of three persons in one God, were there particular aspects that were clarified or reinforced for you? Discuss.

   • You may better acquaint yourselves with some of the roots of this doctrine in the New Testament by reading together from the Gospel of John 14:1-26; 15:26-27; 16:12-15; 16:25-28 and 17:1-5.

_____

_____

_____

_____

_____

_____

Growth in Discipleship

Possible ways to put the themes of this session into action:

- Praying the prayers in n. 227 and/or n. 260
- Meditating on John 14-17
- Praying for greater insight into, and love of, God as a Trinity of Persons

Group Prayers of Intercession

8 to 10 Minutes – Conclude with the Lord's Prayer.

Session 5

The Father Almighty

Reflection on nn. 268-354

We continue to reflect on the first line of the Apostles' Creed: "I believe in God, the Father Almighty, Creator of Heaven and Earth," now turning our attention to the wonder of creation.

Opening Prayer

Come, Lord Jesus,

Bring the fire of your Spirit,

Who is light to our minds and warmth to our
hearts.

Help us to ponder and embrace the truth and
beauty of our Catholic Faith.

May the insights we gain be food for our souls,

Giving shape and meaning to our lives.

Almighty God and Father, we give you thanks for the goodness and beauty of creation, from the morning sunrise to the stars of night, to all the marvelous creatures that surround us. And we praise and thank you for your providential care as we make our way through this world. We know that in every circumstance, even in suffering, "all things work together for good" if we but love you.[1] We thank you for the unseen but glorious world of the angels, especially for those you have assigned to guide and protect us. May they one day lead us home to you.

Amen.

---

[1]Cf., Rom 8:28.

Summary of nn. 268-354

Paragraph 3: The Almighty

Paragraph 3 talks about God as "The Almighty" and explains that his power is always tied to his wisdom, love and mercy. It also touches on the mystery of evil and suffering, which can cause us to wonder—if God is so powerful, why does he allow bad things to happen to good people? But in nn. 272-273 the Catechism reminds us that it was through his cross that Christ conquered evil. Over and over in Sacred Scripture, it is through the weak, the lowly and the suffering that God manifests his power.

Paragraph 4: The Creator

Paragraph 4 discusses God as Creator and shows that a proper understanding of the beginning of the world is crucial. God reveals his love for us through the beauty and goodness of creation. And creation is the beginning of the story of salvation, the story of God's covenants with his people.

The key to understanding creation is provided by the first three chapters of Genesis, which give us perspective on who we are; why and how we came to be; the fundamental goodness and order of the world; how we fell from grace; what destiny God has in store for us.

Paragraph 4 also discusses other aspects of creation, such as the fact that it is the work of all three Persons of the Trinity, and that God continues to hold the world in existence (without which it would simply vanish!). A large section is devoted to God's Providence—the marvelous and mysterious way he governs all things. He does this both directly (himself) and indirectly (through us). In nn. 309-314 we are given helpful insights into the mystery of how there can be suffering and evil in a world governed by a loving God.

Paragraph 5: Heaven and Earth

The first part of Paragraph 5 takes a fascinating look at the angels, who were created through Christ and act as his messengers. Examples of their actions, seen in both the Old and the New Testament, are given in nn. 332-333. They join us in praising God and surround us with their care. Though the Catechism does not mention this, it is worth noting that the Church celebrates two feast days in honor of the angels. The first is September 29th, the Feast of the Archangels Michael, Gabriel and Raphael, and the second is October 2nd, the Feast of the Guardian Angels.

The last part of Paragraph 5 (nn. 337-349) discusses the main truths revealed by God through the Bible's account of the creation of the world—for example, the goodness and the hierarchy of creatures, with man at the summit.

Next session we will look at God's creation of man.

Vocabulary

Omnipotence (268) – Having power over all things, from Latin *omni* for "all," and *potens* for "power."

Filial (270) – Pertaining to or befitting a son or daughter, from Latin *filius/filia* for "son/daughter".

Byzantine liturgy (281) – One of the liturgies belonging to the Eastern Rite of the Catholic Church.

Necessary emanation (285) – A necessary outgrowth of the thing itself. For example, heat "can't help but" emanate from fire and is really part of fire itself. Creation and man are in no way an emanation from God: they are separate, lower realities created by his free decision.

Wisdom sayings (288) – Proverbs or other sayings contained chiefly in the "Wisdom Books" of the Old Testament: Job, the Psalms, Proverbs, Ecclesiastes, the Song of Songs, Wisdom, and Sirach.

First cause (300) – The ultimate origin of all beings. There are many secondary causes in life—for example, the sun is the secondary cause of daylight—but all can be traced back to God as Creator.

Final end (301) – Ultimate purpose or goal.

Physical evil (310) – Disruptions, tragedies, suffering in the physical world (earthquakes, sickness, death, etc.).

Moral evil (311) – The evil of sin, the evil of morally disordered choices. In the end, all physical evil can be traced to moral evil, to original sin and the whole chain of sin that followed. Adam and Eve were created in a world without any physical evil. The moral evil of their pride and disobedience changed that.

Eschatological (326) – An intimidating word that refers to the end of time, the final consummation of history, when God will judge and reign triumphant. The key root is the Greek *eschaton* for "last."

Corporeal (327) – Bodily, material (as contrasted with spiritual). From the Latin *corpus* for "body," as in *Corpus Christi,* or the "Body of Christ."

Precursor (332) – The one who comes before—in this case, John the Baptist.

The Roman Canon (335) – Eucharistic Prayer I, which dates from the sixth century. The various Eucharistic Prayers constitute the heart of the Mass. There are four principal ones, which can be found in a typical Sunday Missalette, but a total of thirteen approved by Rome for use in the United States. Each Eucharistic Prayer begins with the dialogue, "The Lord be with you"—"And with your spirit"—"Lift up your hearts"—"We lift them up to the Lord..." and concludes with the words, "Through him, and with him, and in him, O God, almighty Father, in the unity of the Holy Spirit, all glory and honor is yours, for ever and ever."

At the heart of each Eucharistic Prayer we find the words of Consecration, when the bread and wine are transformed into the Body and Blood of Christ.

Discussion Questions

1. Number 269 affirms our belief in God as the "master of history." If indeed nothing can thwart God's design, his plans, does that mean we are simply actors reciting our predetermined lines in a play written by God? In other words, how can we as Catholics defend our belief in free will in light of our belief in God as master of history?

_____

_____

_____

_____

_____

_____

2. What does the Catechism state is God's greatest display of power (n. 270)? In what moment of Christ's life was it made most evident (n. 272)?

_____

_____

_____

_____

_____

_____

3. Toward the end of World War II, British Prime Minister Winston Churchill cautioned Russian dictator Joseph Stalin to respect the Catholic Church. Stalin scornfully replied, "How many divisions does the Pope of Rome have?" Stalin understood power only as brute force, and the power of Communism seemed unstoppable for decades. But his question was answered in 1989 when the Berlin Wall came tumbling down and Eastern Europe emerged from Communist oppression thanks largely to the influence of Pope John Paul II (along with the unseen power of prayer).

What do we learn from examples like this about the various faces of "power?" From the point of view of the Gospel, name a few of the most powerful men and women in history and describe why and how they were powerful.

_____

_____

_____

_____

4. In number 305 we read: "Jesus asks for childlike abandonment to the providence of our heavenly Father who takes care of his children's smallest needs..."

    •   Why is this attitude of "childlike abandonment" not easy for us?
    •   What is helpful in fostering it? What gets in the way?

_____

_____

_____

_____

_____

_____

5. In nn. 309-314 the Catechism treats the mystery of the existence of evil in a world created and governed by an all-good, all-powerful God. This mystery has troubled many minds and hearts throughout history. Indeed, evil and the suffering it brings are painfully present to all of us. As you read this section, make note of any phrases or ideas that you find especially helpful in grappling with this mystery. Discuss.

_____

_____

_____

_____

_____

_____

_____

_____

6. The Catechism offers us a beautiful reflection on the nature and mission of the angels in nn. 331-336.

   · Discuss what stood out for you from this section.

   · How much thought have you given to the fact that you have a guardian angel?

   · Did you learn the classic prayer to your guardian angel? Probably many people think of it as just a prayer for children to say. What do you think? Pray it together and discuss the kinds of guidance and protection you think God intends your guardian angel to give you:

Prayer to Guardian Angel:

"Angel of God, my guardian dear, to whom God's love commits me here, ever this day (night) be at my side, to light and guard, to rule and guide. Amen."

_____

_____

_____

_____

_____

_____

_____

_____

7. In nn. 339-349 we are given the principles for what we could call a Catholic ecology, or respect for the created world God has placed us in, with its living creatures and natural resources.

List some of these principles, putting them in your own words, and discuss them in the group. How would you compare this model of ecology with the more secular model?

_____

_____

_____

_____

_____

_____

_____

_____

Growth in Discipleship

Possible ways to put the themes of this session into action:

- Praying the Lord's Prayer
- Meditating on Genesis 1:1-31 (creation)
- Meditating on Mt 6:25-34 (God's providence)
- Sharing in God's providence for others through acts of love
- Praying:
  - The Song of Creation (Daniel 3:57-82)
  - St. Francis' Canticle of the Creatures (Excerpted in n. 344)
  - The Prayer to Your Guardian Angel

Group Prayers of Intercession

8 to 10 Minutes – Conclude with the Lord's Prayer.

Session 6

The Mystery of Man

Reflection on
nn. 355-421

We continue to reflect on the first line of the Apostles' Creed—"I believe in God, the Father Almighty, Creator of Heaven and Earth"—now focusing on the creation, fall and redemption of man.

Opening Prayer

Come, Lord Jesus,

Bring the fire of your Spirit,

Who is light to our minds and warmth to our
 hearts.

Help us to ponder and embrace the truth and
 beauty of our Catholic Faith.

May the insights we gain be food for our souls,

Giving shape and meaning to our lives.

O Lord, we are mysteries to ourselves, capable
of greatness yet flawed by sin. This life of ours is
an epic battle between the power of your grace and
the seductions of evil.[1] It was so at the dawn of creation, when Adam succumbed to the lies of the evil
one and the whole drama of fall and redemption
began. It is so today. Thank you for the redeeming gift of your Son, the New Adam, our supreme
Hope and Victor over sin, and of the New Eve, the
sinless virgin who bore him. May we draw close to
them on earth, and be with them in eternity.

Amen.

---

[1]Cf., Romans 7:14-25.

Summary of nn. 355-421

Paragraph 6: Man

Paragraph 6 looks at man from various angles.

He is:

    a. Created in the image of God. This gives him great dignity and the capacity to know and love God, sharing in his divine life, as well as the ability to know and possess himself and to make a gift of himself to others;

    b. A unity of body and soul;

    c. Male and female, thus capable of a special communion of love that leads to the transmission of new life;

In n. 359 we learn that we can only understand man in light of his connection to both the first Adam and the "second Adam," who is Christ. The Catechism explains that the human race forms a unity because of its common origin in these "two Adams."

Paragraph 6 goes on to discuss man's creation in a state of friendship with God, his fall (original sin) through pride and mistrust, and the consequences of that fall for all mankind. Satan's own fall and his role as tempter are also discussed.

In nn. 397-406, the mystery of original sin is addressed. We see that it includes and implicates every one of us because of the "unity of the human race" (n. 404).

Paragraph 6 concludes by pointing out that, from the very moment of the fall, God heralded the coming of a Savior. That Savior, his only Son, would not just restore us from sin. By taking on our human nature, he would raise it to a higher level, with greater blessings than those lost through sin.

Paragraph 7: The Fall

In nn. 385-395, the Catechism gives us the broad outlines of man's fall. It emphasizes the real evil of sin, which must not be rationalized as merely the result of psychological weakness or societal pressures. In the light of God's plan for us, we recognize it rather as an abuse of freedom and an offense against love.

In Genesis 3, the story of the fall is told in figurative language, but it refers to a real event that occurred at the dawn of human history and that has marked human existence ever since. But it is only in the light of the death and Resurrection of Christ that sin and our need of salvation are truly understood. We see what the

Son of God was willing to do and to suffer to save us from our sins. We see at what cost—and with what extraordinary love and mercy—we have been redeemed!

In nn. 391-395, the Catechism reminds us that man was tempted to commit the original sin by Satan, a fallen angel, the "father of lies." (Jn 8:44).

The remainder of Paragraph 7 discusses the nature and consequences of original sin. In a mysterious way, the human race is linked in Adam's sin, and then also in the Redemption won by Christ. Unlike Adam however, original sin is not a personal fault in us, but rather an inherited state of spiritual deprivation in which our minds and wills are weakened and we are inclined to sin. These traits remain even after baptism has cleansed us of original sin. And so this earthly life is a testing ground for which we need God's grace.

Only the Virgin Mary was preserved from original sin by a special grace that also kept her sinless her entire life. She was to be the "New Eve," from whom would come the Savior of the human race, the "New Adam" (n. 411).

Next session we will turn our thoughts to that glorious Savior, as we affirm: "I Believe in Jesus Christ, the Only Son of God."

Vocabulary

The soul as the "form" of the body (365) – "Form," as it is used here, is a technical, philosophical term. Essentially, it refers to that which gives a created reality its substantial identity and character, and, in this case, animates it or gives it life.

"Perfections" of man and woman (370) – Particular gifts, positive attributes, given by God to be appreciated and fostered. For example, a certain kind of masculine courage or feminine tenderness. All these attributes are rooted in God, whom they reflect.

Triple concupiscence (377) – Concupiscence is a disordered attachment or craving. In this case we speak of three such attachments: attachment to sensual pleasure, to earthly possessions and to one's own pride (see 1 John 2:16).

Exultet (412) – A Latin verb meaning "rejoice." The Exultet is an ancient and beautiful hymn which rejoices in our redemption by Christ. It is sung by a cantor (ideally a deacon) after the Paschal candle has been carried forward in procession at the Easter Vigil.

Discussion Questions

1. Much of this session focuses on man's fall, on original sin. But in spite of the tragic reality of sin, the Christian message remains one of joy and beauty.

   As a way of reaffirming this, have someone read aloud the two quotes in small print in nn. 356 and 358.

   What particularly strikes you from these quotes, and why?

   _____

   _____

   _____

   _____

   _____

   _____

2. As Catholics we hold that the human person is a unity of body and soul. We even say that after death we are incomplete until our soul is reunited with our glorified body at the final Resurrection.

   Some other philosophies and religious traditions have held the body to be the prison of the soul, from which the soul must be liberated.

   Why do you think some people would be tempted to see the body in this latter, negative way? What would you point to in Sacred Scripture, in the Catechism, and in your own experience, that supports the Christian view of the goodness of the body?

   _____

   _____

   _____

   _____

   _____

   _____

   _____

   _____

3. Imagine yourself suddenly transported back in time before the fall, before original sin. List the ways in which life would be different (see nn. 374-378). But would something be missing (see n. 412)?

_____

_____

_____

_____

_____

_____

_____

_____

4. Read numbers 386 and 387. When human persons and societies reject the notion of original sin and personal sin, when they fail to see man as fallen and inclined to sin, what consequences follow? And what attitude does that foster toward Christ's suffering and death for us (see n. 389)?

_____

_____

_____

_____

_____

_____

5. Number 397 says of original sin that "Man, tempted by the devil, let his trust in his Creator die in his heart and, abusing his freedom, disobeyed God's command.... All subsequent sin would be disobedience toward God and lack of trust in his goodness."

The disobedience part is easy to see, but how does sin reflect a lack of trust in God's goodness (see Genesis 3:1-11)?

_____

_____

_____

_____

_____

_____

6. We see from n. 406 that the Church's teaching
   about original sin and man's fallen nature walks
   a middle course between the opposite extremes of
   Pelagius on the one hand and the first Protestant
   reformers on the other. In your own words, say how
   this is so.

_____

_____

_____

_____

_____

_____

Growth in Discipleship

Possible ways to put the themes of this session into action:

- Daily examination of conscience
- Avoiding an occasion of sin
- Particular penance or sacrifice
- Praying for growth in a certain virtue
- Encouraging someone who feels hopeless or discouraged
- Prayer of praise and thanksgiving to Christ for his redeeming love

Group Prayers of Intercession

8 to 10 Minutes – Conclude with the Lord's Prayer.

Session 7

And the Word Became Flesh

Reflection on
nn. 422-483

We begin our reflection on the Creed's statement of faith: "I Believe in Jesus Christ, the Only Son of God."

Opening Prayer

Come, Lord Jesus,

Bring the fire of your Spirit,

Who is light to our minds and warmth to our
hearts.

Help us to ponder and embrace the truth and
beauty of our Catholic Faith.

May the insights we gain be food for our souls,

Giving shape and meaning to our lives.

O Lord, you are the Son of God and the King of
the Universe. And yet through your Incarnation
you have taken on our human nature, drawing
"closer to us than we are to ourselves."[1] This is a
mystery too great for us, but full of beauty and
hope. You came down from your heavenly throne
to be born on a bed of straw and to die on a cross,
so much did you love us and wish to save us from
our sins. Knowing you is not only our salvation, it
is our greatest joy. May that knowledge grow ever
deeper, we pray.

Amen.

---

[1]St. Augustine, *Confessions,* III, 6, 11

Summary of nn. 422-483

Introduction

In nn. 422-424 we see summarized the wondrous truth about Jesus Christ: that he is the eternal Son of God, and yet that his Incarnation and mission on earth are firmly inserted in Jewish and Roman history.

The Catechism makes clear that the faith that we embrace and share must be centered on Christ. We must seek to know and love him deeply, and only then are we really able to pass that loving faith on to others (nn. 425-429).

This introductory section concludes in n. 429 by indicating what will come next: first a discussion of the principal titles given to Jesus, then a reflection on the chief mysteries of his life.

"And in Jesus Christ, His Only Son, Our Lord"

Jesus – Christ – The Only Son of God - Lord

This section (nn. 430-451) examines the significance of four names/titles given to our Lord. It is important to understand that names and titles meant far more in biblical times than they do today, often signifying the mission of the person receiving them.

Read and re-read these four reflections slowly and with a spirit of meditation. It would be difficult to find a cluster of paragraphs in the Catechism more packed with meaning.

"He was Conceived by the Power of the Holy Spirit, and was Born of the Virgin Mary"

Paragraph 1: The Son of God Became Man

In nn. 457-460, the Catechism tells us the eternal Son of God became man for four reasons: to reconcile us with God; to reveal God's love to us; to be our model of holiness; and to make us sharers in God's life.

The rest of Paragraph 1 discusses how Jesus Christ can really be true God and true man.

The main points to remember are:

    a. Christ has two distinct and complete natures—human and divine (we might call these natures the "what" of Christ).

    b. The subject possessing these natures is one undivided Person, the divine Second Person of the Trinity (we might call this one Person the "who" of Christ).

    c. In his human nature, Christ has a human soul, intellect, will and body. But Christ's divine nature always shone through his humanity (for example, his human will was always in perfect harmony with his divine will). Still, Christ's human nature also learned and grew on the human level (learning to walk, to talk, to work with tools, etc.).

d. Because the human nature is united with the divine nature in the one Person of the Eternal Son, Christ enjoyed in his human nature an intimate knowledge of the Father and a full understanding of all he had come to reveal (see nn. 473-474).

e. Because of his human nature and body, it is appropriate to depict and venerate images of Christ and of his Sacred Heart (see nn. 470, 478), for indeed, "with a human heart he loved" (*Gaudium et Spes*, 22).

Next session we will continue to study Christ and the "mysteries" of his life.

Vocabulary

The Law (422) – Christ was born under the Law of Moses, the law revealed by Yahweh to the Israelites. This law was "holy, spiritual and good, yet still imperfect" (see nn. 1961-1964). It was brought to completion by Christ, especially in the Sermon on the Mount.

Recapitulate (431) – Means to "go through again" the main points of something. In Christ, God embodies, passes through and brings to fulfillment the Old Testament themes of creation, love, sacrifice and mercy. Christ's merciful love and sacrifice redeems us, making us a "new creation" (2 Cor. 5:17).

Threefold office of priest, prophet, and king (436) – Jesus as Messiah encompasses these three highest roles of Jewish history. As priest, he is the ultimate mediator between God and men. As prophet, he speaks God's truth with supreme authority. As king, he is the eternal ruler and shepherd, but his kingship is one of service and total self-giving, his throne the cross.

Paschal Mystery (444) – "Paschal" is derived from the Greek *Pascha* (from the Hebrew *Pesach*) for "Passover." The Paschal mystery refers to the death and Resurrection of Christ, the definitive Passover Lamb, which saves us, leading us out of slavery to sin and into the Promised Land of new life. The word "mystery" indicates that this is an event that radiates with such profound meaning that we can contemplate it but not fully grasp it. The Paschal Mystery forms the center of the Christian Faith and lies at the heart of every Eucharist. It is celebrated with particular beauty and intensity from Holy Thursday to Easter Sunday.

Discussion Questions

1. Let someone in the group read 1 John 1:1-4, quoted in nn. 425. After a silent pause for reflection, discuss what especially strikes you from this passage.

_____

_____

_____

_____

_____

_____

2. N. 428 states: "Whoever is called 'to teach Christ' must first seek 'the surpassing worth of knowing Christ Jesus'...."

Have you ever heard Christ preached or spoken of in such a way that your heart stirred and you felt inside, "This person knows Christ, intimately"?

- What was it that made you feel that way?
- How do you think a person arrives at that degree of "knowing" Christ?
- What helps, and what gets in the way?

_____

_____

_____

_____

_____

_____

_____

3. Read the accounts of Jesus' baptism in Luke 3:21-22 and John 1:31-34. How was Jesus' "eternal messianic consecration" (n. 438) revealed at that event?

_____

_____

_____

_____

4. In n. 440, the Catechism speaks of two dimensions of Christ's messianic kingship that must always be borne in mind together. What are they? (Hint: Peter was inclined to look for only one dimension—and to be repulsed and scandalized by the other).

_____

_____

_____

5. What especially struck you from the reflection on the four names or titles of Jesus in nn. 430-451?

_____

_____

_____

_____

_____

_____

6. At the end of a discussion of Jesus as "Lord" (nn. 446-451), we see quoted what is nearly the last line of the Bible, the heartfelt cry, "Come, Lord Jesus!" (Revelation 22:20). That cry should echo in the heart of every Christian and every parish community.

   Are there particular prayers, devotions or images that help keep that cry alive in your heart? Are there liturgical or devotional moments or seasons in which that cry seems to come alive in your parish in a particular way?

7. Discuss the four reasons the Word became flesh for us (see nn. 457-460).

_____

_____

_____

_____

8. To what temptation did Adam and Eve succumb (see Genesis 3:4)? How did Jesus precisely reverse that sin (see the quote from St. Paul in n. 461)?

_____

_____

_____

_____

_____

_____

9. Share together your understanding of the manner in which Christ has two natures in one Person. When all is said and done, of course, this is one of the deepest mysteries of our Faith.

_____

_____

_____

_____

_____

_____

_____

_____

Growth in Discipleship

Possible ways to put the themes of this session into action:

- Daily Mass and Communion

- Devotions: Sacred Heart of Jesus, Divine Mercy

- Acts of love for Jesus in your neighbor, especially the suffering and marginalized, for "whatever you did for the least of these...you did for me" (Mt 25:40)

Group Prayers of Intercession

8 to 10 Minutes – Conclude with the Lord's Prayer.

Session 8

Jesus' Birth and Public Ministry

Reflection on nn. 484-570

We continue our reflection on "Jesus Christ, the Only Son of God," turning our attention to the Virgin Mary and to the mysteries of the life of Christ from his birth through his public ministry.

Opening Prayer

Come, Lord Jesus,

Bring the fire of your Spirit,

Who is light to our minds and warmth to our
hearts.

Help us to ponder and embrace the truth and
beauty of our Catholic Faith.

May the insights we gain be food for our souls,

Giving shape and meaning to our lives.

O Lord, the whole of your earthly life is a revelation. It is like a diamond revealing one gleaming facet after another as it is turned and examined. Help us to see with the eyes of faith the profound meaning of your humble birth to a promised virgin full of grace, the hidden years at Nazareth, and your public ministry. May the signs and mysteries we contemplate inspire us with awe and gratitude. **Amen.**

Summary of nn. 484-570

Paragraph 2: "Conceived by the Power of the Holy Spirit and Born of the Virgin Mary."

This section begins with the most extensive treatment of the Virgin Mary in the Catechism. Key Church teachings about Mary are discussed:

- Her *predestination* to be the Mother of Jesus. She was chosen "from all eternity" (n. 488) to be the mother of Jesus. Her coming is foretold even as the first woman, Eve, falls from grace. A series of humble, holy women of the Old Testament point the way to her.

- Her *Immaculate Conception.* Mary is uniquely holy, "redeemed from the moment of her conception" (n. 491), to make her a fitting mother of the Son of God. Full of grace, she would remain sinless her entire life.

- Her title as *Mother of God,* inasmuch as she is the mother of the divine Son according to the flesh.

- The significance of her *perpetual virginity.* In nn. 499-507, the Catechism takes care to explain this mystery, which only "the eyes of faith" (n. 502) can fully appreciate.

Note: Mary's *Assumption* and her role as *Mother of the Church* will be discussed later, in nn. 964-975).

Paragraph 3: The Mysteries of Christ's Life

This paragraph begins by introducing the idea that Christ's whole life is made up of "mysteries." This means that no fact or event in his life is simply ordinary. Each fact or event in Jesus' visible, earthly life is a *sign* pointing to a deeper meaning.

For example, Jesus' birth to a humble virgin in a lowly stable is not merely a "fact," a sort of historical coincidence; no, it is a *sign* to be contemplated, a *mystery*—the mystery of the divinely rich Son of God taking upon himself the poverty of a human nature; also the mystery that Christ invites to the glorious kingdom of Heaven not the proud and self-sufficient, but the meek, the lowly, the "poor in spirit" (Mt 5:3).

The Catechism tells us (nn. 516-518) that everything in Christ's earthly life reveals something about the Father, contributes to our redemption, and recapitulates or *replays* human life (Jesus lives with "straight lines" the life, the human realities, that the descendants of Adam and Eve have only been able to live with "crooked lines" because of sin).

We are called to live out Jesus' mysteries in our own lives. In other words, our lives should trace the pattern of his attitudes, words and actions: loving obedience to the Father, an attitude of humility and gentleness, a spirit of self-sacrifice, zeal for the kingdom of God, etc.

The Catechism then discusses the principal mysteries of Jesus' life in two stages: that of his infancy and hidden life in Nazareth; and that of his public life (beginning with his baptism). Read this section with care, taking the time to contemplate the rich meaning and symbolism contained in each mystery.

Jesus' Infancy and Hidden Life:

- Preparations – Jesus is foreshadowed and announced in the Old Testament and through John the Baptist.

- Incarnation – God becomes man; He who is greatest enters the world in a humble stable.

- Infancy – Jesus is circumcised in accord with Jewish law; revealed to the three magi, who represent the non-Jewish world; presented in the temple, where he is recognized as the Messiah by Simeon and Anna; and taken into Egypt to escape the dark designs of evil that always oppose God.

- Hidden Life – Jesus is obedient to the law and to Joseph and Mary, and for 30 years he experiences and embraces "the most ordinary events of daily life" (n. 533), thus sanctifying all that is good in family life, work and daily affairs.

Jesus' Public Life

- Baptism – Jesus is of course sinless, yet he insists on being baptized by John. He is the sacrificial Lamb who will carry all our sins, and that is symbolized here. The Father and the Spirit are present and active at this key moment.

- Temptations in the Desert – As the New Adam, Jesus faces and defeats the tempter who had brought the first Adam to ruin.

- The Kingdom of God – This is the focus of nn. 541-550. At its core, the kingdom of God is not a particular place, but rather a state of union with God, sharing in his life, guided by his Spirit. It belongs to *"the poor and lowly,* which means those who have accepted it with humble hearts" (n. 544). Jesus' teachings, parables and amazing deeds are pointers and invitations to the kingdom. Who will see, hear and follow?

- The keys of the kingdom – Jesus gives authority to the twelve Apostles, clearly establishing Peter as their head, the "rock" upon which he will build his Church.

- The Transfiguration – Many signs are contained here (Father and Spirit, for example, just as at Jesus' baptism). We see a glimpse of Christ's glory, but with Peter we are reminded that the suffering of the cross must precede the glory of the Resurrection.

- Ascent and entrance into Jerusalem – As he approaches Jerusalem, Jesus is fully aware of the rejection and suffering he is about to face. But his entrance is full of signs that point to his identity as Messiah, glorious yet humble, acclaimed by "children and God's poor" (n. 559).

Vocabulary

Justification (519) – The act of being redeemed from sin, made righteous before God, brought into the state of grace. We are "justified" by the grace of Christ's redeeming death and Resurrection when we are baptized and when, if we have sinned gravely, we return to grace through the Sacrament of Reconciliation. We can cooperate with the grace that justifies us, but we cannot "earn" it.

Enigmatic (546) – Puzzling, mystifying.

Hades (552) – The Greek word for the abode of the dead, the nether world. When used by Christians it generally referred to hell, the abode of Satan and the damned.

Regeneration (556) – Rebirth, the act of entering into a new life.

Daughter of Zion (559) – Mt. Zion was originally the name given to a rocky cliff in what became the city of Jerusalem. In time, the whole city (and even the whole Jewish people) came to be called "Zion," "Daughter Zion," or "Daughter Jerusalem." In Christian usage, the title "Daughter of Zion" is often extended to Mary as representing the faithful poor ones of Israel who awaited and welcomed their Messiah, Jesus Christ.

Discussion Questions

1. Sometimes Catholics are accused of worshiping
    Mary, treating her virtually as Christ's equal. What
    would you point to in this section of the Catechism
    to show that this is not the case—that in fact Mary
    is kept in the proper perspective (see, for example,
    nn. 487, 492, 494)?

    _____

    _____

    _____

    _____

    _____

    _____

    _____

2. The Church teaches that Mary was a virgin not
    only in the conception and birth of Jesus, but
    throughout the rest of her life (she was "ever vir-
    gin"). In seeking to understand the significance of
    this virginity, which of the points in nn. 502-507
    strike you as most helpful, and why?

_____

_____

_____

_____

_____

_____

_____

_____

3. In discussing the "mysteries" of Christ's life, n. 515 states: "From the swaddling clothes of his birth to the vinegar of his Passion and the shroud of his Resurrection, everything in Jesus' life was a sign of his mystery." Discuss the deeper meaning or sign value of the following facts:

- At Jesus' birth he was laid in a manger, which is a feeding trough.

- Jesus lived a hidden and obedient life in a town of no importance for 30 years.

- It was Mary's intercession that prompted Jesus to work his first miracle at Cana.

- When a paralytic was lowered through a roof for healing, Jesus first forgave his sins before healing him physically.

- Jesus' sacrificial death took place at the time of Passover.

- Jesus' risen and glorified body continued to show the wounds of his Passion.

Let each person in your group try to think of one other incident or fact of Jesus' life that is a sign pointing to a deeper meaning.

4. What are the 10 mysteries of the Rosary that medi-
    tate on the birth, infancy and public life of Jesus
    (recall that Pope John Paul II added the Luminous
    Mysteries)? What are a few points discussed in this
    section of the Catechism that might give you more
    food for meditation when you pray the mysteries of
    the Rosary?

_____

_____

_____

_____

_____

_____

_____

_____

5. We read in n. 521 that "Christ enables us *to live in him* all that he himself lived, and *he lives it in us.*" What is the meaning of this statement (read the rest of 521 for help)? What might be a concrete example of it taking place in a person's life?

_____

_____

_____

_____

_____

_____

6. In n. 548 we are told of the many ways people re-
   acted to the miracles of Christ. Go through each of
   these ways of responding and consider how they can
   be applicable to people today, whether in regard to
   Christ's miracles or in regard to signs and miracles
   worked by God in more modern times (such as the
   miracles worked through St. Padre Pio, the heal-
   ings of Lourdes, or maybe something extraordinary
   that has touched you or someone you know).

7. In nn. 554-556, we read of Jesus' Transfiguration and how closely it was linked to his prediction of his Passion and death (See Matthew 17:1-13). What was the lesson Peter and the others needed to learn —and that we must learn—from this linkage (see the small print in nn. 555 and 556)?

_____

_____

_____

_____

_____

_____

Growth in Discipleship

Possible ways to put the themes of this session into action:

The mysteries of Jesus' birth and public ministry:

- Praying the Joyful and Luminous Mysteries of the Rosary
- Meditating on the Gospels, especially related to Jesus' birth and public ministry

Mary, Virgin Mother of God

- Praying the Rosary, other Marian prayers (e.g., the *Memorare,* the *Angelus,* the *Salve Regina)*
- Spiritual reading, recorded talks, etc., on the Virgin Mary

Group Prayers of Intercession

8 to 10 Minutes – Conclude with the Lord's Prayer.

In the next book, Unlocking the Beauty of the Catechism – The Creed: Part Two, *we will resume these reflections, beginning with the mysteries of Christ's Passion and death on the cross.*

The Discipleship Series

Novo Millennio Press